Dedication

I would like to dedicate this book to all that are struggling with mental illness. I would also like to dedicate this book to my family, and the friends that have supported me through this journey.

<u>Preface</u>

In this book, you will discover an in depth look at what it is like to live with mental illness (mostly from my personal experiences). Hopefully, by me sharing my experiences, you will not feel alone, and you will make connections with my stories. I am diagnosed with major depression, generalized anxiety, social anxiety, panic disorder, agoraphobia (where you avoid certain places or situations), and PTSD. For those of you that are "clinically sane", please take a moment to educate yourselves on this topic. This is a REAL illness. Unfortunately, one that is overlooked.

Introduction

My name is Alyssa Aykroyd. I am 26 years old. I know many of you out there are struggling with mental illness. I struggled with my mental illness for as long as I can remember. Half of the battle is knowing where your mental illness stemmed from. Was it genetically inherited? Was it a certain situation that took place in my life? Or could it be a combination of both factors? We suffer in silence, and rack our brains trying to figure out the cause, but rarely can we find an ACTUAL solution. I could not even begin to tell you how many countless hours I have spent asking myself these questions: Why me? Why can't I just be *normal?* Why do I think the way I do? There are more questions than answers.

Chapters

<u>Creating a Monster</u>

"Monsters are real, and ghosts are real too. They live inside us, and sometimes, they win".

-Stephen King

So, let me start from the beginning of my journey through absolute hell. I struggled with this "monster inside of me" for as long as I can remember. I thought my mental illness would get better as the years passed, but it has not, and I still constantly struggle with it daily.

It all stared in Elementary School. I never felt accepted amongst my school mates. I was the girl that never talked to anybody, and always kept to herself. I wore black because I liked it. I never wanted to wear color. It wasn't "for attention" or anything. It was just what I wanted to wear. I was called "goth" for it.

I have always struggled with communication. I could not think of the right things to say, and I felt if I did say something, I would be judged for it. When I did manage to speak (if I was spoken to directly), then I would speak; but I would be so nervous, that I would mess up my words. When I did something such as that, it would ruin my whole day. I was thinking of how stupid I felt, and like I needed a written script just to talk to people. This goes hand in hand with my social anxiety, but I will discuss this in more detail later on.

When I would finally get home from school, I spent my time dreading the next day. I was always questioning what could go wrong tomorrow. I had trouble making friends as well. I managed to make a few friends because I didn't want to seem like more of an outcast than I already was. I remember even as a little girl, getting bullied by boys. One event in particular really stuck with me.

It was a beautiful day, and I was relieved that it was finally recess. I could finally be out of that *prison* for a while, and just forget about my misery. I was swinging on the swing set like usual, seeing how high I could go, (without wrapping myself around the top pole). Suddenly, a boy with short brown hair, and freckles walked up to me with his posse, and told me to stop, so I did. I got off the swing, and suddenly, he started to try to push me to the ground. I defended myself and pushed back. HE was the one who had fell to the ground, while his friends were laughing at him.

That was literally one of the most joyous moments of my life. I had ACTUALLY defended myself. The only part that had really upset me, was when *I* was the one who got in trouble. The supervisor of the playground had only seen *me* push that kid to the ground. So, I was rushed to a room where I had to write my name on a piece of paper repeatedly until recess was over. I was trying to explain the situation to the supervisor, but she did not believe me. Pretty messed up, right?

There is another incident that sticks in my head to this day as well. Yet, another day at recess, I was doing cartwheels, and rounds offs (I was very much into gymnastics). On my last round off, I ripped my pants, and a little kid noticed. It was the same kid that tormented me on the swing set beforehand. He felt the need to point it out to the whole class.

I ran as fast as I could to hide, and found a big oak tree where I just sat there and cried my eyes out, praying to God, and asking him, "why do I have to keep going through this torment?" Even as a little kid, I wanted to die right then and there. To make matters worse, the kid had found me. He called me a cry baby, and I remember saying, "go away, just please go away".

After he felt like he had embarrassed me enough, I stood up, trying my best to compose myself, and got dizzy. For some reason, my vision had gotten blurry. I tried to walk and ended up smacking my head right into the tree. I can honestly say I do not remember much after that. The torment had really never stopped.

Sixth grade was starting to end. Ultimately, I was dreading Middle School because I knew things would get worse; and boy was I right. Middle School is a place where more clicks are involved, and popularity seemed to be more important than anything.

When I was in Middle School, it seemed like the bullying got WAY worse. I was aware most kids did it to show off to their friends. I was still that reserved, "quiet" girl that was dressed in all black. Although, I still had a few friends in Middle School to help me try and stay afloat, (at least somewhat).

I absolutely dreaded gym class, or any group project. I was always the one to be picked last. On a side note, I still cannot comprehend why to this day that teachers allow this. But every time a team that had to take me as the "left over", I would get scoffed at. They had even asked the teacher if they could trade me in, like I was some damaged item. The thing was, I knew I was damaged, but I also was really starting to question my own self-worth.

If it wasn't bad enough that I was embarrassed by the person I was, I became embarrassed by my actions. For example, there was this time where we were in computer class, waiting in the little hallway to the entrance of the main room. Apparently, the computer room used to be a science classroom. There was a faucet on the wall, and I leaned against it. To my dismay, the faucet on the wall broke, and water was flooding everywhere, flowing towards the computer wires and all.

I can at least look back at this story and laugh now about how stupid I was, but in that present moment, I was absolutely mortified. I got called stupid by my classmates, and even the teacher was yelling at me. I literally wanted to run out of the room and never come back. I would like to add that it was school picture day for choir class too, and I didn't have an extra pair of clothes. Always seemed like a case of bad luck, and my stupidity.

You know what comes next. High School. I think everyone especially dreaded that first day of High School. It seemed like you would have to make a good first impression, or else. It was sink or swim. I still was not the type to make good first impressions, or any good impressions at all for that fact.

My first day of High School was so nerve racking to the point where I had vomited before I even got on the bus. I was shaking uncontrollably, my palms were sweaty, and I could barely breathe. It was like trying to breathe under a pillow. The big yellow school bus had pulled up to my stop, and even the smell of the gasoline was making me sick to my stomach. I slowly walked up those steps and was greeted by a nice blonde-haired woman who said, "Hi nice to meet you, and welcome to your first day of High School." More like first day of Hell. I sat in front of the bus because I felt like if I were ever to be picked on, the bus driver would be right there to defend me and put a stop to it. I surprisingly did not have many issues on the bus (probably because people would not recognize I was there) but when we finally arrived at school, it was a different story.

I walked into the doors of the school, overwhelmed by all the people I saw. I absolutely booked it to home room (when I finally managed to find it). And so there I was, sitting quietly in my chair, in my white tank top, with black polka dots, wearing ridiculously heavy black eye liner. I tried to stray away from the black for a day.

My anxiety seemed to catch the attention of the home room teacher, as she asked me, "Honey, are you okay?" And I just said, "Yes I am fine." I did not want the conversation to go on any longer than it had to be.

As the rest of the students took their seats, we were given our welcome speech, received a map of our class locations, and were sent off. I felt like I was being sent off to war. The hallways were the battle grounds. I was given weird looks and was laughed at (probably because of my ridiculous eye liner). Even in the classes throughout the day, the ridicule continued.

There was only one good thing that came out of that first day. In study hall, I was sitting alone, sticking thumb tacks in my fingers because I was trying to distract myself. Suddenly, I look over, and I see a boy with short brown hair and glasses sitting next to me. He said, "Hi my name is Nick." I was so shocked by the fact that somebody was ACTUALLY talking to me. I immediately replied, "Hi, I'm Alyssa, nice to meet you." I was shocked by his next statement he had made to me. He had told me that he stuck thumb tacks in his fingers too. I laughed, and said "Really?" I know it may sound weird to all that are reading this, but it meant a lot to me that somebody was actually making a conversation with me, and we had shared the same weirdness.

We hit it off immediately. We asked each other what classes we had, and even planned on where we could meet up before classes to talk for a bit. He became not only my best friend, but my rock as well. I went to him with problems I was having with boyfriends (yes, I did manage to snag a couple boyfriends) people that were bullying me, and basically just about everything. I saw a lot of myself in Nick. I was so relieved and grateful that I had finally found someone that didn't look at me like a freak, and an outcast. He was having problems of his own too in his personal life but pushed them aside to try and help me.

Of course, the bullying got worse by High School. I was called many kinds of names and was looked at as someone would did not belong. After High School, I have had a couple of instances where people would try to message me via Facebook to try and apologize for what they put me through. I don't know if it was to make themselves feel better, but regardless, I didn't pay it any attention. It actually made me really mad, but at the same time, it was quite comical to me. After what they had put me through, forgive and forget will never be a thought in my head.

Around junior year of High School, there was something that had happened, that was almost like a breaking point for me. I had my first seizure. I was in the computer room, and we were working on some science project. I was about to sit down at the computer when suddenly, my head felt weird. Next thing I knew, I was on the floor, barely conscious, and in a puddle of my own urine. I do not remember much other than hearing faint voices speaking to me, that sounded foreign. I was rushed to the hospital and was slowly regaining my consciousness. I had bruises and scrapes all over my legs, had bitten through my tongue, and felt incredibly weak.

I always described my seizures to be like waking up from the dead. It truly feels like I am waking up to some foreign world that I have never been in. It's hard to recognize my surroundings, and all I can hear are those faint voices, and the sounds of my own breath.

I had a couple of other seizures after that incident as well. I had one on the bus, one at home in bed, and one where I almost fell down a flight of stairs. My parents decided to home school me for a while. To be honest, I

was relieved. It meant not having to go back to that
prison.

I had gone to many various sorts of doctors to find
out what was going on with me, and why this was
happening. I was getting so frustrated by going to so
many doctors, but not having any answers as to why this
was happening to me. I finally went to a neurologist,
and he told me that I have a cyst on my brain that was
basically bleeding onto it. He told me that the cyst was
most likely causing the seizures. To this day, I am unsure
of the actual cause. But luckily, I haven't had a seizure
in almost nine years now.

I guess by this point, with the seizures that occurred,
the bullying, my mental illness in general, the
heartaches, and other contributing factors (that is
unfortunately too painful to even write about), I had
enough. My mental illness had come to a hiatus. I had
become rebellious. I was drinking to get drunk because I
didn't want to feel the emotional pain anymore. I went
years on and off drinking. I was dating guys that treated
me like garbage but staying in the relationship anyways
so that I would not feel alone. There are so many regrets
I have to this day which I feel like I can never get over.

After High School, I went to college full time and was working. College was a whole different scene. No bullies, mostly adults, and I was responsible for myself. Well at this point, I was so wrapped up in my depression, I didn't *want* to be responsible. I did not want to do anything. I honestly don't know how I managed to get through two years. I finally broke down and quit. Part of it was my depression, and part of it was my big fear of driving.

To this day, I still kick myself for making the choices I have made. Not till long ago, I didn't even admit to anyone that I had a problem. I got good at covering it up. I was mostly ashamed, and fearful of being judged. It took me awhile to even go to my own family about my problems. Even though I knew they would support me, I still had a fear in the back of my mind of being judged. I have been trying to connect the dots myself for so long. It gets frustrating having all these questions, but absolutely no answers.

Going to present day, I am doing everything in my power to try to improve myself. I have been seeing a psychiatrist, finally went to that doctor's appointment that I put off for years, landed a good job, and now have a counselor. I have also been losing weight, which was a big struggle for. Stress eating was another bad habit of mine. I managed to reach 250 pounds. I am now glad to say I am well below that. Before losing weight the right way (good old diet and exercise), I was completely doing it wrong.

I started to lose the weight by eating little to no food each day. Sometimes, I would go days without eating. I was so ashamed of the way I looked. I wore baggy clothes to try to conceal it. I wouldn't dare put on anything like a dress, or any type of fitted clothing. I was ultimately too ashamed to even look at myself in the mirror.

In this period of time, I had moved to New Hampshire to go live with my boyfriend. He also had depression and anxiety. He said I needed to lose weight, so I didn't do it by my own will at first. I wanted to make him happy. It felt like he did everything to try and change the person I was, so I would be to his liking. I would feel ignored by him, and unloved. I moved my whole entire life for him and left my family in Connecticut. I hate to say it, but I do give him some credit. If he didn't tell me to lose weight, I would still be that 250-pound girl. I found it odd that in that period of time, I was using my insecurities to motivate me. He also did suggest going to a counselor. But his answer to everything was "just take a pill," instead of being there for me (emotionally) when I needed him the most.

For the longest time, I hated myself for moving away from my family too; they are the only people that are actually there for me and love me. I was missing my nephew and niece growing up, family events, and time overall with family that I can never get back. I absolutely went down the rabbit hole then. I don't know why I feel the need to stay in toxic relationships. Maybe because I feel like it is what I deserve? I was just looking for someone to genuinely love me for me.

When my mother got sick with severe ulcerative colitis, it threw me down into an even deeper depression. She also had come down with an infection that covered the entire inside of her body. The doctors gave her a 10% chance of living. At this time, I had a full-time job in New Hampshire still, but I left my job to move back to Connecticut to see my mother. I didn't know if she was going to make it. I never would have forgiven myself if I weren't there for her. I could not even go into the hospital at the time because of COVID-19 pandemic.

Miraculously, and I mean MIRACULOUSLY, she was doing better. After a while, she had come home. When I first saw her, she was so weak. It broke my heart. I wanted to be there to take care of her. Luckily, today she is recovered, but it has been a rough journey.

So now that you guys and gals have a clearer understanding of my roots, and the struggles I have been through, I am going to dive into the struggles, and daily challenges of my mental illness. I honestly, still to this day, have a hard time talking about it. Luckily, I don't have to talk about it, I can write about it.

Anonymous Anxiety

"I have anxiety about anxiety, then I worry the anxiety will ruin my life. It's a snake-eats-tail loop. But in opening up to others, I found a lot of people have felt the same way."

-Rachel Bloom

My anxiety (especially social anxiety) has been one of the biggest downfalls for me. It comes out of nowhere, and I have no control over it. It truly feels like you are running from a monster that you cannot get away from.

From school, to working, or even going to the grocery store, it has been a constant internal battle. I look at the outside world like a vicious lion who is going to attack me. And Sometimes, I have panic attacks about having a panic attack.

Every time I must encounter people, I stare at the ground, try not to make eye contact, and occupy myself by mostly music, or staring into my phone. This is my way of saying "don't talk to me." I cannot put my finger on why I have such a hate for people, and why I can only see the bad over the good.

Even when a person does manage to talk to me (disregarding my earphones), the conversation ends quickly. My brain gets scrambled, and I cannot process my words, or thoughts. I get the dreaded awkward silence, and essentially, word vomit comes out.

My mind gets so wrapped up in, "what am I going to say next to embarrass myself?" It is the fear of judgement, and my inability of producing actual words because my brain is going 1,000 miles a minute. I have such this hate for people, but yet, I still care what people think about me. Makes sense, right?

Going to work, I used to be a Customer Service Lead for a hardware store. I was trying to give myself some, what you call, *exposure therapy.* I dealt with people all day, every day. I thought by facing my fears and talking to all kinds of people, that I would eventually get rid of my fear. Unfortunately, that was not the case.

I always had people yelling at me over things that were out of my control. Some people are fortunate enough to just "brush it off', but it is completely different with me. It can, and most likely will ruin my whole day. Maybe it reminds me of the times I was bullied in school for my anxiety; something that was out of my control.

I do not know how I managed to stay at my job for almost four years. Every morning I woke up knowing that I had to go back, and it was absolute torture for me. I would physically get sick and vomit. I would shake uncontrollably and struggled to breathe. I felt so nauseous; almost as if I were on one of those crazy roller coaster rides, except there was no stop at the end of the ride. I was sweating, and my hands would literally go numb from cramping up. It was like school all over again.

For those of you who have panic attacks, I am sure you can relate. It is one of the most devastating things we can go through. The worst part is that *we* have no control over it. There is no on/off switch.

I pushed on like this for years because I did not want to be considered a "failure". I put my mind and body through absolute hell, but yet somehow managed to put on a facade. I knew it was my job. It was my livelyhood. How I promoted myself to a "Lead" is still baffling to me till this day. All I know is that I did my job, and I did it well. I always tried to just submerse my mind on work, and not the people. I think that it was a distraction, and almost like a coping mechanism for me. I believe it to be the reason why I did not quit.

I ended up transferring stores from Connecticut to New Hampshire to go live with my boyfriend. We had a major age difference, but it did not really matter to us. I wanted to be there with him. He understood mental illness. I ultimately moved because he was undergoing surgery, and I wanted to be there for him. After a while, he went through his own period of depression. He laid in bed for months on end.

It was difficult for me in terms of trying to be there for him when I was struggling with my own mental illness. But every time I would come home from work, I would just lay in bed with him. Even on my own birthday, all I did was come home from work, order a small pizza for myself, and laid in bed with him.

What I have learned is you cannot help others fully until you can help yourself. I may have been there for emotional support, but I couldn't help him fully, as I was fighting my own battles.

Going back to transferring stores, working in a new place with unfamiliar faces made matters worse for me. Not only did I have a new workplace, I was living in a whole different state. I guess the "unknown" and "unfamiliar" is what really bothers me. But I took the risk because there was someone there who needed me. My counselor always tells me I need to stop helping others before helping myself. To me it seems selfish, but also makes sense. We cannot help in carrying a load when our arms are broken.

So, I went into my new store, anxious as all hell, and was greeted by the human resources representative of the store. He was also my personal tour guide. When he was showing me around to meet my new co-workers, I awkwardly said my "hello's", and quickly moved onto the next one. I was a little comforted by the friendliness that was presented.

As time passed, they recognized my skills, and I was always offered various positions that were high up in the chain. In the time I was there, it felt good to me. I liked helping my associates and being knowledgeable about everything. But there were still *people* involved in the mix. In general, people even just being around made me extremely uncomfortable, but the rudeness (mostly from customers) that carried on put me over the edge.

With both locations I worked, I can honestly say it really felt like I was in school all over again. I ate lunch in the bathroom most of the time because I needed a break from people. I needed my own time to try and recollect myself, face the music, and get back on the floor.

The bathroom upgraded to eating in my car, eventually. Even in extreme temperatures, I wouldn't dare turn on the car for heat or air conditioning because that would attract attention to the smokers outside. I liked when it snowed because the snow would cover up my windshield. I was comforted by the fact that no one would be able to physically see me. I was hidden from the outside world, in my own little snow globe. Even if it meant I had to endure extreme temperatures, a half hour of peace was worth it to me.

There are so many different types of anxieties and panic disorders. I tend to struggle mostly with generalized anxiety, social anxiety, and panic disorder. With panic disorder, it is like all my fears are being thrown at me, all at once. It feels like I am literally dying, and the walls closing in on me. It is another vicious monster. It grabs me, and it seems like it will never let go.

It seems as though a panic attack is the big bomb that gets dropped on me, and my anxiety that follows throughout the course of my day are the grenades being

thrown. That is why I say it is like a constant battle, and
I do not want to send myself off to war.

I have always had trouble in adapting to the outside
world. I realize the world can be a beautiful place
sometimes. But with mental illness, the world around
me turns grim. I don't want the feeling of panic to
overcome me, and I will surely avoid it at all costs. I
will talk more about this in my next chapter on
agoraphobia.

<u>Hide and Go Stay Hidden</u>

"Choosing to live in narrow spaces leads to form of mental agoraphobia and that brings its own terrors. I think the willfully unimaginative see more monsters, they are often more afraid. What is more, those who choose not to empathize enable real monsters. For without ever committing an act of outright evil ourselves, we collude through our own apathy. "

-J.K. Rowling

While agoraphobia stems from panic and anxiety, it is ultimately its own "monster". One that can lead into depression. It is like a never-ending game of hide and go seek. I am hiding from the world, and I am seeking solitude. I take comfort in the walls of my own home. I avoid going places that I know will cause me to panic or to be fearful. Agoraphobia ties in with my vehophobia (sometimes called amaxophobia), which is the fear of driving, or even being in a vehicle. I do not have the fear of riding in a vehicle per say, but I do have a deathly fear of driving.

I could not tell you where my fear of driving came from. I have never been in an accident, I have never seen an accident that traumatized me, nor have I just flipped on the T.V. and saw an accident in a movie scene that had triggered me. The minute I started driving, was the moment I had become fearful of it. It is another case of "this should not bother me," or "why can't I just be a normal young adult?"

When I get behind the wheel, I am in absolute panic. I get the same side effects as mentioned before. I get physically sick, my hands start shaking and become numb, I start sweating, and my heart feels like it is beating out of my chest. Of course, anyone would fear an accident, but that is not particularly what is running through my mind. It is the physical action of driving. When I do manage to "get myself on the horse" so to speak, and I almost encounter an accident, my panic sets me even more.

This phobia has ruined a lot of things for me. It has been ruining my life. Agoraphobia, amongst many other of my mental illnesses, is the reason why I stopped attending college. It got to a point where I eventually had to drive myself. I absolutely hate myself for it, and there's not a day that goes by that I regret it. I was too embarrassed to admit to anyone that I had this phobia.

Agoraphobia has not only ruined my educational pursuance but has put me through a lot of hardships. It made me sick to my stomach when I had to go to work and made me want to avoid work all together. But I did it anyways because I knew I had to.

Before going to work, I would just sit at the kitchen table, smoke my cigarettes, drink my morning coffee, and keep an eye on the clock. With every second that struck, I knew I was another second away from having to hit the road. I am aware that this fear may sound absolutely ridiculous to some, but I have come to realize there are many other people out there with the same fear. I am not alone.

When I was finally able to step into my vehicle, before running to the bathroom to vomit, I drove. And on my drive, I would have to pull over to try to compose myself, and vomit even more. The best way to describe this fear is like almost driving off the edge of a cliff. I feel like I am on the edge of my own sanity.

I have lost many friends, and close connections because of this phobia. Every time I was asked to meet up somewhere to go hangout, I was always sick, busy, or fell asleep. There are only so many times you can use such excuses. But I felt as though the excuses were easier to tell than the truth. I was embarrassed of my fear, and afraid of losing my friends; as well as all the other close people in my life, such as my family. So, eventually these people (except my family) took it as I just simply didn't want to hang out, I didn't value our relationship anymore, or I was plain uninterested.

I get so aggravated over the fact that I cannot completely conquer this fear, even with trying "exposure therapy". It has costed me a lot and makes me question my own self-worth. It is taking ahold of my life. I wish so badly to just be able to snap my finger, and it would vanish. But life doesn't work that way unfortunately.

With agoraphobia, I avoid leaving my home at all costs because 1know I am safe here. I don't want to risk having a panic attack or going out in the public to see crowds of people. From time to time, when I finally muster up the courage to go out, I almost immediately regret it. It is a cycle and will keep me from attempting to go out again. In the past, I have avoided going to the doctor's office, and have been reluctant in going to seek psychiatric help because of this phobia.

I am currently living in this terrible Corona Virus pandemic. I am hesitant to say that in this crisis, I am relieved about some things that have come out of it. For one, it gives me even more of a reason to not have to leave my home. Secondly, appointments are still being held virtually. This is the reason why I have finally been able to see my doctor, psychologist, and my psychiatrist, amongst other things I would not have done if I had to physically go somewhere.

I always ask myself, "why can't I just go out places"? I recognize the beauty in the actual world around me, and I am aware that there are some good people out there. Unfortunately, in my case, I have experienced more bad than good. I see everyone else going out, hanging out with friends, and it makes me feel worthless that I cannot do these simple things.

I remember one particular incident at a diner my parents brought me to. We were coming back from a camping trip in Rhode Island (I didn't mind camping much because it is more secluded.) And we stopped at this little diner not far from my home in Connecticut. When we pulled up to the diner, my heart felt like it was in my throat. I saw a line out the door. I immediately began to panic. That same feeling came across me; I knew this was a bad idea. I went into the diner anyways because I did not want to upset my parents. As soon as we walked in, I was literally shoulder to shoulder with a bunch of these random strangers. My heart began to race, and I began to shake uncontrollably. I turned to my mom and asked her if we could get out of there. She asked "why?" And I screamed at the top of my lungs in anger, "it is too crowded in here." Everyone turned around to look at me and I wanted so badly to just sink into the floor. After begging my mom to leave, she finally gave in and they walked out. I RAN out hysterically crying and trying to push people out of my way. I immediately got back into the car where I was safe. These types of situations make me never want to go out again. It is a vicious cycle.

Agoraphobia has always been one of the most challenging mental illnesses I face. Most times, people catch me just staring out the window. They believe me to be spacing out, but in reality, I am imagining myself taking that leap and going into the outside world. Like the saying goes that "eyes are the windows to the soul", I feel as if windows are just a false hope to an outside world that I cannot be in.

Diving into Depression

"Depression is a prison where you are both the suffering prisoner and the cruel jailer. "

-Dorothy Rowe

Depression is one of those mental illnesses that words simply cannot do justice. It is dark, grim, and you feel as though you are diving into a bottomless pit. It is like you are in a tunnel; you can see only the darkness that resides, but not the light at the end of it. Billions of people suffer from situational depression. They either have lost a loved one, lost their job, or became ill (to list a few). It is stressful events in one's life that onsets the depression. I don't believe there to be a single person out there who has not experienced this type of depression at some point in their lives.

I suffer from major depressive disorder. It is like losing that loved one, losing a job, or becoming ill every single day. It doesn't come and go. It lingers. It is not like seasonal depression where the season changes, and things are back to normal. Depression is like a demon. It picks and preys and lives inside of you. It sucks all the happiness out of you, takes any bit of light you had left, and tum it into an infinite darkness.

An ongoing depression can affect not only one's emotions, but physical well-being. It can lead to heart disease, obesity, diabetes, Alzheimer's disease, and other chronic disorders. The survival rate is low because of the depressed person's willingness to get the treatment they need.

There are not many stories I can tell about this illness in particular because it is a never-ending story, and it comes out of nowhere (I will leave that up to my psychologist). I also find that my other mental illnesses usually all have conscious triggers, whereas my depression just hits me like a tidal wave and throws me to the bottom. It is like a thief in the night.

Depression lead me down the road to my drinking for quite a while. I did not want to feel the emotional pain anymore. Even if it meant only being out of my head for a couple hours, it was worth it to me. I wasn't the "bar room drinker" per say. Instead, I purchased my own bottles from the liquor store not too far down the road, and I brought it up to my room with me. No one joined

in my drinking escapades. It was only me, and my four
walls.

I am glad to share with you that I am not that drinker
I once was. It may have been a temporary solution to me
at the time, but eventually, I came to find out it was not
a permanent one. I saw what it has done, and has been
doing to those around me. I did not want to self-induce
myself in another illness that I would have to face. That
is one of the few things I feel like I have done right in
my life. I was being self-destructive. I am still self-
destructive today, not through my drinking, but through
my actions.

When I have something good going for me, I
somehow manage to ruin it all the time. Is it because I
am not feeling worthy of my own accomplishments? Or
like I wouldn't deserve the happiness that would come if
I actually followed through? My bad decision-making
didn't come until later on in my life because I believe I
bottled up my depression; so much to the point where I
felt like irrational behavior was the answer. I think anger
has a lot to do with it. I am angry that there is no relief. I
am angry over past traumatizing events that have
happened in my life. How easy it would be if I could just
let go of the past.

My depression also caused me to gain weight as well. I felt like eating was an escape. I was trying to fill a void. At this point, I did not care what I was doing to my body. I was treating my body like a garbage disposal. I suppose I can say losing weight was another thing I feel like I have done right by, but I'm afraid of falling down that hole again.

As I continue in my deep depression, I continue with a hopeless state of mind. I don't feel like I have a sense of worth. I question if life around me is just a figment of my imagination because I don't want it to be real. If I could create my own reality, it wouldn't be anything like this one. All I want is happiness. Happiness with myself, and happiness with life in general.

A huge part of depression in self-esteem issues; physical or emotional. On a physical aspect, I do not see the beauty in myself; even when people say otherwise. It was first about my looks. I didn't believe my facial features were physically attractive. That is why I caked my face in makeup and tried my best to hide it. I thought the more that I put on, the better it would conceal my actual face. I ended up looking ridiculous with the mismatching concealer, and heavy eyeliner. At least I can look back at myself now and realize that.

So, all in all, I have gained a little more confidence throughout the years. I don't feel the need to wear makeup. And i f I do, it is a small amount. As uncomfortable as it makes me, I have been trying to stick with the notion of embracing my natural beauty. Again, it is a method of exposure therapy. As hard, and as uncomfortable as it makes me, I still always try to push myself. I never stop trying to fight.

I mentioned my issue with weight previously. I continue to push myself in exercising (almost) every day, or even just eating less. Even though I dread it, I still do it because I am hoping in the end, I can have a self-image that I can be proud of. It is one less thing I can be ashamed of. I wouldn't have to wear the black, baggy clothes anymore. The issue is, I like to take things to extremes. I will do anything to get to where I want to go, even if it means harming my physical and emotional state. And in the end, I will end up crashing and burning. It is self-sabotage, and I can't seem to find an "in between".

(Me as a Teenager)

(Me in Present Day

Another major component of depression is restlessness; whether it means not being able to fall asleep, stay asleep, or oversleeping. Ever since I was a little kid, I had trouble with falling asleep. For countless years, every single night, I had night terrors. It was so bad, that it came to a point where I wasn't able to sleep at all. The only time I managed to get somewhat of a decent night's sleep was when I got to sleep in my parent's bed.

I remember having dreams about all sorts of monsters, demons, and people trying to kill me. It seemed like I could never get a break from the night terrors. I am ashamed to admit that not till a couple years back (I am now 26), I finally managed to sleep without the lights on. It is normal for children to have bad dreams, but not to my extent. I look back today and wonder that how, even as a little kid, my mind could create up such horrible events.

It got to the point where I did not even want to sleep. I did not want to wake up in absolute terror. But eventually, my brain would shut down from the lack of sleep, and I would have to face my night terrors again.

I have seen things to this day (more so as a child), that would probably enable people to call me a schizophrenic. I hesitate when talking about the subject because of the ridicule, and not wanting to be classified as something I am not. You cannot deny what you see with your own eyes; physical spirits, and objects being thrown. I believe it to be the cause for my re-occurring night terrors.

As an adult today, I luckily do not have any more of these night terrors. Now, I just have trouble sleeping. I can lay in bed with my eyes closed for hours, and still nothing comes of it. It is so frustrating, and I have tried everything under the sun to help me, yet still nothing comes of it. I have to mentally exhaust myself just so I can get some sleep.

What I have noticed is I can never stop thinking and worrying. No matter how hard I try to keep my mind in the "present moment", it always seems to wander to past and future events in my life. My mind attempts to go to a place where most people in general would find relaxing. Countless times, I have tried to imagine myself on a beach, relaxing in the sun. Suddenly, it is like the dark clouds roll in, and it is back to the raging storm of thoughts in my head. My mind physically imagines that scene in particular. The sun suddenly washes away and is only left to darkness.

I do not know if the reason I have trouble sleeping in present day has any relation to my night terrors as a child. I do not fear dreams of monsters, demons, or being killed. Instead, I feel the "monster" has finally overtaken me, and no one is killing me but myself.

I suffer the physical consequences of my lack of sleep. Of course, being mentally and physically exhausted. I also feel my brain cannot process too much information, and I get overwhelmed easily. I have tried to hide the dark circles under my eyes with makeup, but even makeup can't fully hide it.

To this day, I still wonder if my lack of sleep was a trigger for my seizures. I feel like if my brain can't properly function, it can go into overdrive. It can offset the electrical activity in my brain. Again, it always seems like I have more questions than answers.

I remember in High School, most times, I would be sitting in study halls with my MP3 player, just listening to "Mad World" by Gary Jules on repeat. That song to me exemplified the exact way I was feeling.

Depression affects me and so many other people in different ways. What I think affects me the most about depression, and the millions of people out there is the actual feelings that comes of it. The feeling that you are worthless, that there is no hope, and every day is grim. We wish so desperately that we can just go out and enjoy everyday life, but we cannot see the sun behind the clouds. We are stuck in a deep hole that we cannot get out of.

Finding the Cause of PTSD

""Traumatic stress cuts to the heart of life, interfering with one's capacity to love, create, and work - incapacity brought on not by poor lifestyle choices, moral weakness, or character flaws but by a complex interpl$_{ay}$ among biology, genes, and environment. "

-ShailiJain

For the longest time, I have been trying to find the root of my PTSD. It has been the biggest mystery to me. I am trying to fmd the exact "why". I unknowingly avoid certain situations such as going out in public around a bunch of people or having a simple conversation with someone.

I do not know where my PTSD specifically stemmed from. When I look back at my life, I consider the bullying that took place, and the people that have hurt me. To this day, when a school bus goes by and I smell the stench of gasoline that emits from it, it makes me sick to my stomach, and I have a panic attack. I believe the bullying that occurred in the life has made me have a distaste and distrust for people overall.

People often have a misconception of PTSD for someone who has explicitly served in the military and has seen or experienced a traumatic event that had occurred during war. This is not the case. PTSD can be caused by ANY traumatic event that has occurred in a person's life. Flashbacks, nightmares, uncontrollable thoughts, and anxiety can occur with PTSD. Anything that appeals to the senses: sight, sound, touch, taste, and smell, can trigger one's PTSD as well.

It seems like I have a warped conception of the people around me because of various events that happened in my life. Because of that, I tend to avoid situations, unknowingly. I don't really have any "flash backs" that have occurred, and that is why it is so puzzling for me to figure out the cause.

I have been trying to put the pieces together myself. There are probably even more memories in my life that my brain has physically blocked out. I found that blocking out such memories or events is the brain's coping mechanism. It doesn't want to re-live those memories. It more so gets swept under the rug.

I've been doing some research on "inner child therapy". It is a form of therapy where you try to bring yourself back as a child. It basically explains that the "child within" has never left us. Multiple different techniques are used such as putting yourself in your own shoes as a child, meditating on certain memories of past events, and telling your inner child that everything will be okay. What I fear most is bringing up those repressed memories.

I have been told by my therapist that I have a fear of fear. I always think of the things that could possibly go wrong. To be honest, digging up those painful memories doesn't sound appealing to me. I would rather keep it swept under that rug.

Another trigger that I find confusing is being startled by loud noises. While writing this, a phone just ran next to me, and I went into a panic. My heart felt like it dropped in my chest, and I had trouble breathing. Loud, unexpected noises frighten me. I did not realize this just until recently.

The confusing part to me is that I can watch jump scares, and horror movies all day long, and not flinch. Maybe it's because my mind is recognizing that the movie is not reality, and I am expecting it to have "jump scare" moments. It is the unexpected and unknown that seem so startle me, and the fact that I am not living in a movie, but rather real life.

I believe that my PTSD is what led me to having angry outbursts. If I feel uncomfortable in a particular situation, or I feel hurt, I will have an outburst of anger. Even when someone says something to me that is not really considered "hurtful" to most, I instead get defensive, and I have a burning range, feeling like I must defend myself. I have a high sensitivity level that I cannot control.

But the door swings both ways. Sometimes I feel the need to apologize for things that weren't even remotely related to me. I always get a weird look from people as they say, "this has nothing to do with you, what are you apologizing for?" I feel like Jekyll and Hyde sometimes. Maybe each memory or suppressed memory that I am associating with is mirroring my mood and mirroring my reaction to what had occurred in my life.

I cannot always relate situations to my reactions, and the reason as to why I may have had those reactions. If I had to make a comparison, it is like asking me what an object is from a far distance (having poor vision) without a way to see. I can vaguely make out the shapes and colors, but I struggle to see what the actual object is. I have clues as to what it may be (given the shapes and colors), so my brain tries to relate it to a familiar object

with the same qualities. With my PTSD, I have the
memories that I can actually remember, and try to
connect it to my everyday actions and reactions. When it
comes to the memories I suppress, I feel as though I am
just blind, and can't make any connections at all.

Everyone is different when it comes to symptoms of
PTSD. Everyone has had different experiences,
reactions, and lifestyle choices because of this disorder.
PTSD has not just specifically derived from one who has
had a traumatic event happen to them in their life.
Sometimes, it can even be genetics. And sometimes,
there is not even a reasonable explanation as to why
someone has PTSD.

That is why this disorder is so difficult to
comprehend. Now and again, it will even leave
therapists scratching their heads. Without a reasonable
explanation as to WHY someone has PTSD, it is hard to
treat. It is like trying to find the cure to an unknown
virus. We don't understand the virus, and what will kill
it off. We can only study it and make observations until
we can hopefully find the solution, or at least help
manage it.

<u>Ending Thoughts</u>

"That's the stigma, because, unfortunately, we live in a world where ifyou breakyour arm, everyone runs over to sign your cast, but ifyou tell people you 're depressed, everyone runs the other way. That's the stigma. We are so, so, so accepting o fany body part breaking down, other than our brains. And that's ignorance. That's pure ignorance. And that ignorance has created a world that doesn't understand depression, that doesn't understand mental health. "

-Kevin Bree/

I always question why society in general is always so quick to have empathy for a person with a physical disability, but usually disregard a person with mental illness. Just because our brain cannot be physically seen, doesn't mean the wounds are not there. And people question why sometimes people with mental illness do not get help.

Primarily, we get judged. And if we finally mange to open up about it, we get remarks such as "you will get over it" or "just think positive." It is a pure lack of understanding. For those who are mentally disabled (dealing with depression), they usually struggle with the idea of wanting to get help. We are in a state of mind where we simply won't bother because we either think it will not help, or we feel so far down the rabbit hole, and there is no way to escape.

It took me the longest time to finally seek out therapy, and medication management. I am still in my beginning stages of my healing process. So far, I have honestly seen some improvements in myself. You could not even get me to talk about my mental illness before. I was mostly ashamed, apprehensive about judgement, and thought it was a phase I would soon get over. I am now beginning to believe there may just be a light at the end of that tunnel.

The most important thing to recognize is that we are not alone. I have spent countless days and nights reading articles about people with the same disabilities I have. I take comfort in knowing that someone out there understands what it is like to experience this mental madness. I also empathize with them because I would not even wish mental illness upon my worst enemy.

It is true when they say, "there are strengths in numbers." Just even recognizing the fact that there are people out there like me gives me a little more hope. I recognize that I still have a long journey ahead of me in fighting this internal battle. I will admit, there are days where I feel like giving up. I realize the only true failure in life is not trying, and this does not only apply strictly to mental illness. If you mess up a task at work, you don't call it quits and storm out of the building. You correct your mistake, and you learn from it. Even if you keep falling, you have to get back up because who knows if you will ever even get back up again.

There has always been a link between mental illness and creativity, specifically in the arts: writing, music, art, and more. Some of the most famous painters, such as Vincent van Gogh struggled through his life with manic depression. It ultimately led to his suicide. In one of his last letters he wrote he said: "If I could have worked without this accursed disease, what things I might have done."

One of my favorite poets, Edgar Allan Poe, suffered from recurrent depression, and bipolar disorder. He also abused alcohol, and drugs. This was all believed to be the ultimate cause of his death.

I remember in High School reading this poem called "Alone", by Edgar Allan Poe. It has really stuck with me to this day. His poem expresses how he felt going through depression as a child. Edgar Allan Poe was one of the few people to guide me through my expressive outlets. I began writing a lot, drawing, singing music, and even learning some piano. There was a lot of his life that I felt like I could connect with.

I believe these creative outlets to be like another coping mechanism. I for one, found it to be a distraction as well. My biggest outlet is poetry. I can let my words flow freely, not having to worry about the paper judging me. It is like a therapy in itself.

In school, creative writing class was also an escape for me. Although, there were times where we had to read our poems out loud in front of the class (which was absolutely mortifying). I would get laughed at, scoffs, and weird looks from my classmates.

The following is Edgar Allan Poe's poem "Alone". I think about this poem from time to time, and like I mentioned before it has always stuck with me. It is hard for some of us (especially me), to verbally speak out the way we feel, so instead, I write poetry.

"Alone"

By: Edgar Allan Poe

From childhood's hour I have not been

As others were - I have not seen

As others saw - I could not bring

My passions from a common spring -

From the same source I have not taken

My sorrow - I could not awaken

My heart to joy at the same tone -

And all I lov'd - 1 lov'd alone -

Then - in my childhood - in the dawn

Of a most stormy life - was drawn

From ev'ry depth of good and ill

The mystery which binds me still -

From the torrent, or the fountain -

From the red cliff of the mountain -

From the sun that 'round me roll'd

In its autumn tint of gold -

From the lightning in the sky

As it pass'd me flying by -

From the thunder, and the storm -

And the cloud that took the form

(When the rest of Heaven was blue)

Of a demon in my view -

One of the thoughts I have been pondering upon is if there is a link between these mental illnesses. And the question of if a person that has mental illness can be at risk of developing another? Taking my experiences for example, my anxiety, social anxiety, panic attacks, PTSD, and agoraphobia could have led to my depression.

If I sit back and think about it, having these mental illnesses ultimately make me feel unworthy, or give me a sense of not belonging. Specifically, with my anxiety, I get depressed because I feel like my anxiety overtakes me, and there is nothing I can do about it. I also think to myself, "this is something any *normal* person would not be upset about."

My issue with PTSD also depresses me because of certain memories that I do remember pop into my head, such as being bullied as a child. It is like I am re-living the daunting experiences all over again.

Agoraphobia is almost as depressing as depression itself. The fact that I cannot go out like a *normal* person to even the grocery store makes me feel less. The fact that I cannot drive a car without having a panic attack also depresses me. I wish so badly to muster up the courage to go out and have a good time.

On the other side of the coin, sometimes, I will have no reason to be depressed. It just hits me like a ton of bricks. Concludingly, there is not sure-fire answer as to if there is a definite link between my depression and my other mental illnesses. Although, many scientific studies have shown that depression and anxiety commonly occur together. There may or may not be a correlation to all my mental illnesses. It is difficult to pinpoint with so many factors at hand. Either way, each and their own are a recipe for disaster.

Sometimes, I feel like it is not always beneficial to try to figure out the actual causes and possibilities as to why I have these mental illnesses, and where they stemmed from. If I constantly kept trying to find the actual *real* cause to my problems, I believe it may drive me to insanity.

Each mental illness, and the people that are associated with them is unique like a snowflake. Not one snowflake is alike. Each has their own shapes and patterns. Ultimately, they are all still snowflakes. We are all the same and have to form together like a snowball.

We all remember having snowball fights as a child. We would get such satisfaction out of picking up that snow in our gloved hands and forming the snowball we would use to hit our victims with. The tighter you packed the snow, the harder that snowball would hit. Well guess what? We can become that snowball.

If we all stick together, we can become stronger, and try to pack a powerful punch. If you stay hidden behind the snowbank, one of two things will happen. The opposing force (mental illness) will sneak up on you and attack, or you can wave the white flag and call it quits without even taking a shot. You let the enemy win either way.

We have a better chance of defeating the *monster* if we stick together and recognize there truly are strength in numbers. It is important we build a support system and try to get the help we need. Do not wait until it is too late or be led to the false fact that this is an illness which will someday go away, like I have done.

Many of these mental illnesses lead to suicides because the people that are struggling, believe there is no way out, and there is no way their life can get even just a little bit better. They are again, in a hopeless state of mind.

I will go back in saying, you truly are not alone. There are many people out there in the world like you and I, or even a friend you many know. It is important that we all recognize the seriousness of mental illness. It is time to consider this an actual ILLNESS. The best we can do is try and form together in unity and seek out some form of help.

I love all of you. And believe me when I say, I know how you feel. And for those of you who are "clinically sane", I hope I have given you some informative insight on what mental illness is like. This way, you can be more understanding of those around you struggling with this. We need more love in this world. Take care of yourself, and others.

<h1>Resources</h1>

Websites:

www.mentalhealth.gov/talk/people-mental-health-problems

www.talkspace.com

www.heretohelp.be.ca

www.psychiatry.org/patients-families/helping-a-loved-one-cope-with-a-mental-illness

www.emotionsanonymous.org

Phone Numbers:

1-800-950-6264 (NAMI)

1-866-615-6464 (NIMH)

1-800-273-8255 (National Suicide Prevention Lifeline)

<u>Notes</u>

www.ingramcontent.com/pod-product-compliance
Lightning Source LLC
Chambersburg PA
CBHW051415250726
48655CB00003B/1066